IMAGES OF ENGLAND

Farnham
by the Wey

IMAGES OF ENGLAND

Farnham
by the Wey

Jean Parratt

NONSUCH

Hatch Mill, situated where the River Wey flows just a few yards from the Farnham bypass near Hickley's Corner, has been used for a variety of purposes including fulling, as a laundry, a dairy and currently as a store for theatrical costumes. This picture from the Borelli Collection looks idyllic but it was probably far from being an easy life, working in a dairy before the days of electricity and running water. It is also interesting to note that the only person working is the woman – the men are just watching her.

Dedication

For Guy Bellamy, author, journalist and a hard, but fair taskmaster, who gave me the confidence and encouragement to write, and for Ilse Lentz, a dear friend and courageous woman.

First published 1995
This new pocket edition 2006
Images unchanged from first edition

Nonsuch Publishing Limited
The Mill, Brimscombe Port,
Stroud, Gloucestershire, GL5 2QG
www.nonsuch-publishing.com

Nonsuch Publishing is an imprint of Tempus Publishing Group

British Library Cataloguing in Publication Data.
A catalogue record for this book is available from the British Library.

ISBN 1-84588-272-5

Typesetting and origination by Nonsuch Publishing Limited
Printed in Great Britain by Oaklands Book Services Limited

Contents

Introduction

Farnham has been home to men, women and children for longer than any other place in this country. From the time that families from the Mesolithic period dug pit dwellings at a site, close to the present sewage treatment works near the Six Bells roundabout, right up to the present day, evidence suggests that there has never been a time in the last 8,000 years that this sheltered place, with a river for water, gravel for flint tools, wood for firing kilns, clay for making pots, good soil for growing hops, and on a major route between the coast and London, has not been inhabited by human beings.

On the whole it has also been a peaceful place with only the odd hiccough of unrest, such as during the time of the Danish invasion (when legend states that Farnham women protected the town from the enemy, from a vantage point in the Parish Church) and during the period of the Civil War. It has also been a place where philanthropy abounded and many of the men who made vast sums of money through business either ploughed it back through such places as almshouses or used their wealth and position to influence planners and other such bodies into retaining the best of past centuries so that they could live on into the future – with the notable exception of what many people believe to have been the desecration of part of East Street, to build The Woolmead, in the 1960s and early 1970s.

One of the best examples of people banding together to keep an old building for the benefit of the community was shown over the purchasing of a derelict maltings building, in Red Lion Lane. On 11 January 1968, the *Surrey and Hants News*, then a broadsheet, weekly paid-for newspaper, carried a front-page lead story under the headline "Bid To Save River Buildings." It referred to an attempt by a Farnham councillor, Lieutenant Colonel Morgan Bransby-Williams, to persuade his colleagues on the council to give serious consideration to preserving a block of seventy-year-old riverside buildings, once owned by Courage Brewery, which had been left standing derelict for ten years.

Within a few weeks over 500 people crammed into the hall at Farnham Grammar School, in Morley Road, and all swore unswerving loyalty to the cause of preserving the nineteenth-century building. The Farnham Society, under the chairmanship of Dr. A. Crowe, organized the meeting and in a publicity booklet, Dr. Crowe, who died in March 1995, wrote: 'Farnham was a market town, supplying the surrounding countryside and processing its products. With its fields and meadows at the bottom of the gardens of the houses it was itself part of the rural world. Its small population shared rural habits, knowledge and tastes and lived by peasant rules of decorum. Work was hard, skilled and local, and provided the common bond of the community.

'This has changed. A good centre for shopping is not a market town. Farnham is becoming a town and the bond is no longer work but residence. We work forty miles around and come home to...what? Our biological functions? Our hobbies?

'Why choose Farnham to live and sleep and eat in? Perhaps it's convenient for working in some parts of London or the Home Counties. Maybe it's the cheapest spot on this particular circle of the commuter belt. Maybe it's easy to get out of it. Whatever the reason that people are choosing to come here Farnham is becoming a town, with all the problems of town life.

'Modern towns suffer from the fact that by and large people do not choose to live in them. People live in them by force of economic circumstance. This is especially true of the English whose romanticism makes them kid themselves to the last possible moment that they live in the country. In the past ribbon development, the ultimate expression of this self-deception, led us to ruin the country without building towns. We now do this by other devices and it is time we recognized that we are urban people and that living in a town offers advantages as positive as living in a village.

'A town offers the possibility of common enjoyment. This was the essence of town life in the past. The town could offer public buildings in which music could be made by professionals or serious amateurs, where plays could be performed in a worthy setting, and where treasures that no individual will ever possess could be shown. A town offered places of meeting and talk.'

Dr. Crowe continued giving reasons and examples of why Farnham needed a building like the Maltings and concluded his article thus: 'Let's have a little style, a little quality in our lives which can lead us to understand each other in spite of age or class. Let's use the Maltings.'

His plea was heard and from that moment many of the people of Farnham took the mammoth task of preserving the building to their hearts.

Over the period of its history Farnham has had many 'characters' – people who are just a little bit out-of-the-ordinary but who have left their marks in a variety of ways in the tapestry which makes up the fabric of the town. From the early 1920s until the late 1950s Harold Falkner, the architect, was possibly the best known. Whenever a building was demolished he stored the bricks, wood, tiles and even complete shop fronts in order to use them again, either to make a new building appear older or to enhance a building with something good which was being taken down elsewhere.

Another such character was Annie Martin, a Londoner, who came to Farnham at the outbreak of the Second World War and started a greengrocery stall at the foot of Castle Street. She always called a spade a spade, did not mind whether she offended or pleased with what she said, but always made certain that those in need were helped. Until she was well into her eighties she cooked beetroot every weekday, in a huge copper behind her home in Long Garden Walk, then, when it was ready she would catch any passer-by she could see to: 'Just nip down the stall and tell 'em the beetroot's cooked.' I was on my way to a funeral one day, just before Christmas, when Annie's rasping voice rang out ordering me to deliver the beetroot message. It was no use giving an excuse, such as a funeral, for not doing her bidding so I had to run but I am possibly the only person in Farnham, en route to such a ceremony, who has had to perform an errand like that.

Although William Cobbett, author, radical, Member of Parliament and founder of *Hansard*, who is, arguably, Farnham's greatest son, was never able to attend school because of his family's poverty, most children in the town have had good opportunities for education both in the state and private sectors. Both Farnham Grammar School, founded over 400 years ago and its sister, Farnham Girls' Grammar School, much younger but nonetheless equally good academically, have produced men and women who have excelled in all major professions but particularly in careers involved with the written word. One former pupil, Ron Ridout, who died in 1994, holds the record for being Britain's most successful writer of textbooks. He had had 515 titles published since 1958, with sales of 91.35million. His book, *The First English Workbook*, sold 5.6 million copies.

Before education became compulsory for all children, the more wealthy families in Farnham had a good choice of private educational establishments to which they could send their offspring. Churches of various denominations also provided children with a sound foundation of the 'three Rs', but in some cases, such as at Hale School (founded by Bishop Sumner, Bishop of Winchester, who lived in Farnham Castle), if children attended day school from Monday to Friday it was also compulsory for them to attend Sunday School on the Sabbath.

A town as old as Farnham can, quite naturally, boast a lordship which is described as 'one of the most ancient and important Saxon lordships in England.' The first record of the title appears in a charter of 688 AD and, until recently, it has been held by the Bishops of Winchester. The famous St Swithun held the Lordship of Farnham and, in 858 AD he granted some of the manorial land to Ethelbald, King of the West Saxons.

Today the title, which was bought at auction in London in the late 1980s, is held by Ken Kent, a local property developer who was born in Aldershot but has lived in Farnham for most of his adult life.

Farnham hops were, at one time the most expensive in the world and were much-prized for their subtle flavour and light colour. The proximity of Farnham to Aldershot (the Home of the British Army), and the fact that before Aldershot had its own railway station troops had to travel to Farnham by train and then walk to their camp, resulted in a rapid increase in public houses to cater for the soldiers' thirsts Farnham was said at one time to have had more pubs per head of population than any other town in the country.

Farnham has also had its fair share of 'firsts' besides being the site of the oldest village. The first traffic offence to warrant a fine was committed in Castle Street and it was in this street, too, that the first two-minute silence was observed. It is the town in which Toc-H was founded, where the man who originated Daylight Saving was born, where Talking Newspapers for the Blind began and where Mike Hawthorn was brought up and educated and the town to which he brought the World Motor Racing Championship to Britain for the first time.

Many national authors have lived and written in Farnham including Izaak Walton, J.M. Barrie, Dean Swift, William Cobbett and Alfred Lord Tennyson of the past to Ken Follett, Frederick Forsyth, Joanna Trollope and Guy Bellamy of the present, but perhaps it would be fitting to end this introduction with some words used by Arthur Mee in his *The King's England* series: 'Even if Farnham were not, in itself, a spectacular and historic place it would be captivating for its setting, for the magnificent natural country at its doors.'

Farnham, by the Wey, is a place more steeped in history and with more ghosts than anywhere else in this country. I was not born here but it is the town I have adopted as my home. Despite its many drawbacks, not the least of which is traffic congestion, early on a Sunday morning in autumn, when the weak sun shines on dew-covered cobwebs in the hedges where wild hops still grow, and where the castle can just be seen on the hill through the mist, it would be hard to find anywhere more peaceful and beautiful than this country town in a river valley.

One

Over the Rooftops

Ever since man's first flights in aeroplanes, the people left on terra firma have been fascinated to see what their homes and gardens looked like from the air. It is also a way of getting town layouts into perspective and offers an opportunity, today, for potential land developers to find 'hidden' plots of land in which to build homes or an office block. Most of the photographs in this section have only been taken from vantage points above ground, like the Parish Church, but one was taken in the early 1930s, by the airborne parent of a child at Barfield School, which was then situated in Upper Hale Road.

Eddie Trusler, a press photographer, spent a number of hours in the early 1950s, taking photographs of places in Farnham which he, with a newspaperman's ear to the ground, knew would not continue to exist for much longer. Today, Farnham Police Station stands on this site which is a view from Longbridge towards the Parish Church of St Andrew. John Mills & Sons built many houses and shops in the town and the villages beyond in their heyday, but as can be seen, only the sign remained by Easter 1954, with the odd bits of brick and wood which can be seen being purely rubbish.

The upper picture on this page is one from the previously unpublished Borelli Collection and shows Firgrove Hill looking towards the town, and was probably taken in the late 1920s when houses were few and traffic sparse. The lower photograph, taken at least two decades earlier, looks from Farnham Castle, across the town in the valley, towards the Ridgway (the spot from where the above picture was taken). The tall chimney of Knight's Bank is visible as is the building in The Borough which has been a bank since 1865. Additions to it, at the western end, were constructed in 1904, and, although the date of this photograph is not known exactly, it must be before 1904 because there are only three bays on this bank building (there are now five) which faces the foot of Castle Street.

A sign on the lamp standard points to 'Ladies and Gents Lavatories', when the conveniences were situated to the right of the Council Offices in South Street. Postcards of this building, showing the entrances for the respective sexes, had the words 'ladies' and 'gentlemen' painted out before the card was mass-produced because it was thought that such intimate notices could restrict sales of the card. The buildings on the right, including Heath's Cycles and Shrubb's Photographer, were demolished in the early 1960s and the first phase of the current complex, known as The Woolmead, was opened in 1966. Traffic is no longer allowed in both directions on this road and the Royal Deer, in the foreground, closed as a pub at the end of the 1980s, to exchange real ale for Adam's ale, when Mid Southern Water took over the premises as its offices.

The photographer of the picture on the previous page must have snapped his camera only seconds earlier to record the view above because the same Morris Minor car can be seen in both views. The Southern Gas Board building was probably the most mourned of all the East Street premises which were demolished to make way for The Woolmead. Although the gas showroom is so well remembered it served this purpose for less than 30 years, before that time being three shops, Davies' newsagents, Pomfret's confectioners and a fishmonger and poulterer's unit.

Standing gravestones, skipping children and stationary cars mingle between the rooftops of this view taken from the Parish Church in the mid-1980s, when Elphicks departmental store in West Street had recently expanded. During this conversion the old stables, where the horses, which pulled the delivery carts for the Farnham Dairy were kept, were demolished.

When work was being carried out on the Town Hall buildings at the foot of Castle Street, in the late 1920s, this photograph was taken from the top of the building. In the foreground, right, is one of the chimneys of Knight's Bank. There were two and one is now on the Bush Hotel. The other faces W.H.Smith, from the Town Hall Buildings. This is another of the views in the Borelli Collection and was probably taken on a Sunday morning in spring because the blinds are up on the windows of Tily and Brown, the hardware shop, and there are no signs of hop poles in the gardens at the back of the picture.

The Parish Church of St. Andrew can be seen in the distance and in the foreground of this picture are hops, growing up poles, and by their height it is probably early July. The photograph was taken from a vantage point at the castle and the original is in the archives of the Museum of Farnham.

Above: Farnham town centre once had a number of oast houses but today few remain. However, there is one to the side of Hone's at 49, Downing Street, and this was photographed in the snow soon after the end of the Second World War.

Left: Farnham Workhouse, in Hale Road, was not a place to invite the skills of many photographers. It can be seen here, though, as the long dark roof which has a tall chimney to the right of it. Two women sit on the seat, in Farnham Park, just a few months before the end of the Second World War, and while they chat they are looking out over the rooftops of their homes in Park Road.

The Hop Blossom public house connects the two photographs on this page, although they were taken about 80 years apart. Above, 'The Hop' as it is known locally, can be seen roughly in the centre of the built-up area and the view was probably taken from the roof of St Andrew's Church. All the area on the left is now either built upon for houses and shops or is used as a car park. Farnham Castle can just be glimpsed at the back. Farnham once had hop grounds which stretched as close to the town as the backs of the shop buildings.

In this view over rooftops, but looking in the opposite direction to the picture above, the Hop Blossom public house is in the centre once again. The rafters which are in the foreground form part of the roofs of the Lion and Lamb Yard complex of shops and offices which were built in the mid-1980s, mainly on the site of Wm. Kingham's former warehouse. The narrow thoroughfare leading through to Castle Street, in the distance, was once a rope walk with the product made being sold in Tily and Brown's ironmonger's.

It was dangerous to cross the road at this point at Hickley's Corner, even in 1972 when this shot was taken from a vantage point in The Fairfield. Father and child wait by the traffic lights for the road to clear but great care was still needed to be taken at this black spot which has claimed many lives since the bypass was constructed. Ashley Terrace in the centre, was demolished to make road widening possible. The remains of a wartime defence bollard can be seen bottom right.

It only needed a turn of about forty-five degrees to the right for the photographer to take this second view at Hickley's Corner. The building once housed Hickley's the ironmonger, which later became Doulton, Bournes and Doulton. It was eventually demolished to widen the bypass at this point and thus to make it even more dangerous than it was in 1972. Abbey Street was a thoroughfare and the way which monks used to take into town when they were en route from this country's first Cistercian Abbey which was built at Waverley (on the Elstead Road), to see the Bishop of Winchester in Farnham Castle.

There are far fewer buildings in Farnham than now, in this aerial view which was probably taken in the late 1930s. The old gas works can be easily distinguished by its round shape, on the right, and the keep of Farnham Castle is the round area on the extreme left. The fields on the left are those on which the hops can be seen growing in an earlier picture in this section. Where the road forks towards the rear right, The Albion public house is visible and the fields at the extreme right were those in which the 'Forces' Sweetheart', Vera Lynn, (now Dame Vera Lynn) spent her happy, childhood holidays before the Second World War. What was then West Street Boys' School is the building complex on the left.

In 1933 the Oast House Preparatory School for Boys, owned by Thomas Griffith, was opened in The Oast House, Upper Hale Road (the large building in the centre). The house had belonged to the Milroy family and 35 years earlier had been a lace school for young ladies. When the boys' school first opened it had just two pupils, one boarder, Danny Campbell, son of Colonel Campbell and a day boy, ? Vere Brown, the son of a Farnham bank manager. The fees were modest, £25 per term for boarders and day boys paid between £8 and £12 per term, depending upon their age. The roll increased gradually and by 1936 one of the pupils, whose father was in the RAF, took some aerial photographs of the school, as can be seen above. One of the football goalposts is visible, bottom left, and at the top of the photograph is Hale Vicarage, at that time occupied by the Rev. Pastfield. In August 1936 the pupils and staff moved to a new location at Runfold and took up occupancy of Barfield, the former home of John Henry Knight, inventor, author and a photographer of the highest calibre. At Barfield one of the school's most famous pupils was Michael Hawthorn, who grew up to be Britain's first World Motor Racing Driving Champion.

Two

Back to School

For many children in the past, school-days, which should be really happy if any learning is to be achieved, were times of abject misery. Beatings were commonplace, even for slight misdemeanors, such as kicking a football on to a roof. The annual visit of the school inspector brought fear into the hearts of child and teacher alike, when the latter's pay was determined by the former's knowledge. In Farnham, however, there were a number of enlightened educationalists and although some of the following pictures show children who were seen and not heard, in the main they project the youngsters enjoying themselves at the same time as learning.

When the Oast House Preparatory School moved from Hale to Runfold, and was renamed Barfield Preparatory School, the boy pupils were in their element. There was now much more space in which to run around. The brick wall, built by an automatic wall-building machine invented by John Henry Knight, could be seen in the school grounds and there was plenty of room for an old hay wagon, given by farmer Jim Tice in 1958, which was a source of learning and, inevitably, was used in games connected with the wild west. The boys were expected to help renovate, and keep in good condition this part of Farnham's history and can be seen here busy with paint brushes.

The caps worn by the small boys at Miss Stroud's school at 78 West Street look somewhat like those worn by Wolf Cubs, younger members of the Boy Scout Movement, from the 1930s to the 1980s. The building in which the school was held still stands and is opposite to the Surrey Language Centre. It is interesting to note that these young boys, photographed a century ago, have been symmetrically posed and that Miss Stroud, rather than 'watching the birdie', seems to have her eyes fastened on a possible miscreant.

Children at The Park (which had earlier been known as East Street) School, performed a nativity play for parents and friends in December 1975. Joseph was played by John McAndrew and Maria Clark was the Virgin Mary. Others in the scene are Jamie Rose (the Angel Gabriel), Gary Wolverson, Stephen Cracknell, Nicky Fry (shepherds), Gary Farr, Ralph Emerson (kings), Tracey Warren, Lisa Greengrass, Verna Carey, Karina Hayden, Samantha Dodd, Sara Culver, Sarah Dixon (musician) and amongst the well-disguised centurions is Mark Ferguson.

Opposite: A mile away from Miss Stroud's school, stood East Street School, where many of the children who attended were very poor. Amongst the children who can be seen outside the building which was known as 'the top school' because it was farther up St James's Avenue than the 'big' school are: Eileen Hobbs, Joyce Smallbone, Ray Firmin and his twin brother, Harold Harrington and Frank Roberts who, in later life, ran a highly successful leather goods shop in East Street.

Above: The Bishop of Winchester was kept busy in Farnham during May 1909, laying both the foundation stone for the new Wrecclesham School (until that time the schoolroom had been a corrugated iron-roofed hut), and for the new Church House in Union Road, next door to what was then the police station. The *Surrey and Hants News* produced a special supplement to take in both events with the photography being covered by a local man, G.Hale.

Left: Many schools relied on the church for their founding and upkeep so it is only natural that religious education played a big part in the curriculum. In 1897, the year of Queen Victoria's Diamond Jubilee, young Lottie Nash passed 'a specially satisfactory Examination in Religious Knowledge,' and her certificate was signed by three dignitaries, the Bishop of the Diocese, the Diocesan Inspector, and the Rector, the Rev. W. Herbert Moody.

For many years St George's School operated from a large Georgian house in Castle Street. The school, however, had insufficient space for a cafeteria on the premises so the youngsters used to walk, two-by-two, to a Chinese restaurant in Downing Street, for their midday meal. They wore grey coats and grey hats and caps with a red motif of St George slaying the dragon. The school moved to larger premises at Pierrepont, Frensham, and then, in 1994, moved yet again to the campus of Frensham Heights co-educational establishment at Rowledge.

Children at play in St Polycarp's School playground when the school was situated in Bear Lane, next door to where the former Catholic church stood in Farnham and opposite to the Drill Hall which was demolished for the St Georges complex.

Boys will be boys, is a common saying, and the lads at West Street Boys' School lived up to that reputation – in the nicest possible way. Reggie Tipton, extreme left in the middle row, was a self-taught pianist whose skills were renowned in the area and Bobby Sherfield started the Maxi School of Motoring when he grew up. John 'Dixie' Cloonan, left, back row, became a plumber and others in this picture include Stan Winslade, Bobby Court, Bobby Alcock, Richard Nicholls and Ronnie Matthews.

In 1917 the girls at Farnham Girls' Grammar School were educated in the former Boys' Grammar School building in West Street. These five friends used to meet on the Shortheath Road each day and then cycle together to their school. On the way home they went via School Hill, Wrecclesham, so that they could watch Mr Trodd, the blacksmith, shoe horses. The girls are Lois Wilkinson, Winnie Tilberry, Ena White, Marjorie Furlonger and Kathleen Howlett, all in their regular clothing rather than their school uniform, which included a straw hat which 'grew' from the centre every time it became wet.

This team of beaming young sportsmen come from Wrecclesham School and are posing with their headmaster, Mr Bunting, centre, and master, Mr Case, right. The school later became known as St Peter's School and Mr Case finished his teaching career by helping adults at evening classes as opposed to small boys and girls in primary school.

In the Fathers *versus* Sons cricket match at Barfield School on 15 July 1939, the young players, in typical prep. school style – to be known only by their surnames – are Bridge, Davison, Somers Cox, Ford, Clissol, Benson, Halliwell, Goddard, Greathead, Murray and Hawthorn, who was out for four. It might seem that young Michael Hawthorn, right, front row, was to fare better behind a racing car wheel than behind a cricket bat. He later won the title of Britain's first World Motor Racing Driving Champion.

There are just two men among the many young ladies who can be seen here at Farnham Girls' Grammar School *circa* 1970. Mr Betts, the caretaker, is on the right in the second row from the front. Other staff in the line-up include Miss Champion, Mrs Honnick and Mrs Tonkins. The girls, most of whom are sporting longish hair, and managing, as their predecessors did not, to let it hang loose rather than be tied back with pieces of string (as was former teacher Miss Basford's punishment for such a transgression), were obviously having trouble with the wind, which would appear to have been blowing quite strongly. The FGGS moved from West Street to a purpose-built school in Menin Way, a short time before the start of the Second World War.

Three

That's Entertainment

Farnham has been fortunate to have had cinemas, theatres, church halls and open spaces where plays, films, pageants and both schoolchildren and adult groups have given polished performances; albeit the players mostly only had amateur status. Music has long played a part in entertaining people of all ages and the town has a number of choirs, music societies and both traditional and modern jazz groups who perform anywhere people are willing to listen to them, including the Maltings, the stage of which has seen performances by professional musicians performing from all parts of the world.

This modern jazz trio played regularly in a restaurant at the top of Downing Street, during the late 1970s. Tony Nuttall is the string bass player and Alan Leishman, at that time a sub-editor with the *Aldershot News*, is the alto saxophone player. Alan, his wife, Jan (also a journalist) and their two children, emigrated to Australia in the mid-1980s. On acoustic guitar is Ted Parratt, an author, journalist and in the latter role a former editor of the *Surrey and Hants News* series. He is also well-known in local jazz circles.

This building was knocked down to make way for the St Georges development, between Bear Lane and Castle Street, a group of flats, offices and town houses, constructed as part of Kents Developments, Ken Kent being Lord of the Manor of Farnham. St Georges does not have an apostrophe in the proper noun of its name — much to the consternation of local historians and journalists. The building here was once a cinema, and, according to the Kinematograph Year Book for 1913, when it was called the Farnham Picture Palace, its seating capacity was 450.

Weybourne Women's Institute put on many plays for the benefit of the local community and in the 1956 production, which was a thriller, two of the actresses were Mrs Doris Downham, seated and Mrs Gladys Bowdery, right, in the rôle of a French detective.

Above: Had it not been for the Second World War, the Castle Theatre might never have come into being. In 1939 a travelling company of actors, en route from the continent to London, stopped off in Farnham for the night and found a unit just off Castle Street which had once formed part of the silent cinema seen on the previous page. They decided to stay in this town, formed the Farnham Repertory Company and the rest is history. This intimate theatre was so tiny that patrons often put their feet up on to the stage while they watched plays and it was not unknown for a smoker to get up and stub out his cigarette in a prop ashtray on the set (smoking was allowed in theatres in those days). Sir Michael Redgrave said that this theatre was the most haunted of any in which he had played.

Right: Audrey Henderson, right, was a journalist on both the *Surrey and Hants News* and the *Farnham Herald*, who spent many happy hours reviewing plays at both the Castle Theatre and its successor, the Redgrave Theatre. She wrote *Exits and Entrances*, tracing the history of the Castle Theatre, and its ghost, Rotca, and left Farnham in the mid-1980s to work on a newspaper in Brighton.

When Farnham's Regal cinema (latterly known as Studios One and Two) was suddenly closed down in 1985 the townspeople were up in arms. It had been built 52 years earlier, had been opened by a Bishop and was the only large art deco building in the town centre. In its early days, afternoon tea could be enjoyed on the first floor, with customers dining at Lloyd Loom, glass-topped tables with chrome corners and sitting on Lloyd Loom chairs. Other pictures in this book show the final hours, in 1987, of this much-loved building, which has not been replaced by anything (other than an area of rough ground for a car park with grey hoarding boards around it), in the eight years since the cinema's demolition by Bass plc.

There will be very few readers of this book who will recognize Vera Welch, from Thackeray Road, East Ham, London, the child in this picture which was taken in Weybourne. However, once told that in later life she was known as the 'Forces' Sweetheart' there will be very few people who will not recognize the name of Dame Vera Lynn. In her autobiography, *Vocal Refrain*, published by W.H. Allen in 1972, Dame Vera tells of her love for Farnham. Every year, from her youngest days, she spent a month at Weybourne, about a mile from Farnham town centre, with her mother and brother, Roger, staying with her Auntie Maggie, Uncle George and cousin Georgie. Dame Vera wrote: 'My memories of those holidays in Weybourne are amongst the most precious things I possess, and they have coloured my whole life. They are somehow a part of whatever I am. At every moment of stress or discomfort in my life, I have been able to draw on them, like the time in the unbelievable, sticky heat of Burma, when I suddenly remembered the cool taste of water taken from a well near Weybourne.' The young Vera remembered Vi Mason's shop (which stood at the crossroads of Upper and Lower Weybourne Lanes and Weybourne Road), and the walks across the fields for lemonade outside the Six Bells. She later bought her first car, a green Austin 10, cabriolet top, registration number HV 8777, at a cost of £200. She was eighteen years old at the time and one of the first journeys she made in it was to Weybourne, 'partly because I wanted to show off and partly because I couldn't wait to be back there,' she wrote. When she was married and had a daughter, Virginia, she still returned to Farnham but, with more money in her pocket she stayed at the Bush Hotel, a place for which she, her husband and Virginia have fond memories.

Above: In 1949, one of the country's most popular music hall stars, Jessie Matthews, visited the old people in St James's Homes in Hale Road, and was featured in the *Farnham Herald*. They are pictured in front of the newly-built Roman Way estate of post-war houses. Jessie was, for a time, licensee of The Alliance public house at the top of Downing Street, and later bought a house at Weybourne which she called Evergreen. Like Vera Lynn, Jessie was also a customer at Vi Mason's shop at Weybourne. The Six Bells pub which Vera Lynn remembered going to as a child, can just be seen at the back, left.

Left: Jessie Matthews in 1943, pictured on a piece of sheet music. After her singing and dancing career ended Jessie was best-known for her portrayal of Mrs Dale in the long-running BBC radio serial *Mrs Dale's Diary*.

A happy occasion at the Castle Theatre with W.H.Talbot (in spectacles) restraining the gentleman on his left – could he be admonishing him for smoking?

Princess Margaret visited the Redgrave Theatre for a gala performance in June 1984 exactly ten years after she had attended the theatre's official opening. To her right is Paul Keyworth, a Farnham businessman who was also on the board of directors of the Redgrave Theatre and to Mr Keyworth's right is Tim Flood, who was the theatre's manager at that time. Tim's daughter, Charlotte, who was three years old, presented the Princess with a bouquet before the performance that evening.

Above: The second pageant to be held in Farnham in the twentieth century, took place at Farnham Castle in 1930. Its producer was Mrs Bernard Limpus, who lived at Shakespeare Cottage, Shortheath. At the end of the pageant the performers gave her a brown, leather-covered album, with a silver plate on the front, filled with photographs of the event. Miss Ceinwen Roberts, seated, was the lady harpist in the episode concerning The Royal Baby at the Castle, an incident which took place in 1486. Miss Evelyn 'Jo' Simmonds, from Eugene Fuller's Studio, was one of the official photographers of the event, which was performed to raise money to save Farnham Castle, which had been unoccupied since 1927 and was in drastic need of repair.

Left: In the incident mentioned above, the young Prince Arthur, who was described as a sickly child but one who flourished while staying at Farnham Castle, was played by Master Jeffery Barnard (as he was billed in the programme). In this snapshot of the sixteen-month-old 'prince' he looks far from sickly and must have been quite heavy for Mrs E.Barnard, his mother, who played the part of the prince's nurse, to carry around throughout the run of the pageant in July 1930.

Four

Work, Rest and Play

Currently the manufacturers of a famous chocolate bar state that their product is supposed to give one energy to work, rest and play, but in the past, when the majority of the photographs in this section were taken, that piece of confectionery had yet to be invented. However, the men, women and children who can be seen on the following pages, seemed to be able to exist without its sugar, chocolate and glucose, yet still to have had plenty of energy to apply to many interests and activities.

The River Wey has been a playground for children ever since man settled in its valley. In this picture from the Borelli Collection, the children relax against a backdrop of Hatch Mill. It was probably summer because the child in the foreground is wearing a sunhat. The other children are all wearing hats, as well, though, despite what is probably quite a warm day. It would seem likely that the photographer posed the children before clicking his shutter because they are spread so well around the picture and the folded arm position was, presumably, to stop movement spoiling the finished photograph, which is most likely to be about 90 years old.

There can be little doubt that football was a popular game in the Goolding family, judging by this line-up of the Farnham Town Football club in the 1930/31 season, with front row, left to right: A. Brade, F. Harrington, V. Spooner. Seated: A. Varney, S. Goode, R. Clements, P. Saunders, E. Aldred. Standing: G. Vass (linesman), -?- A. Loving, J. Skuse, C. Goode, J. Kimber (hon. secretary), G. Goolding (captain), B. Goolding, F. Goolding (president), A. Hancock, N. Goolding (treasurer).

Who would have dared to argue with the decision of any judge dressed as formally as the gentlemen in this picture, who were the adjudicators at a sports day held at Broomleaf Farm in the first decade of the twentieth century? Broomleaf, near the station, was used for sporting events and The Fairfield, close by, was where, as the name suggests, travelling fairgrounds set up their rides. It was hoped that train passengers, seeing the sideshows, would alight at Farnham, and visit the fair before travelling on to Bentley and Alton.

Riding bicycles on grass and wearing long skirts could hardly have been the easiest of pursuits, which is possibly why it was considered to be worthy of a competition at the Broomleaf sports day. The ladies do not appear to have skirt guards on their back wheels, either, which must also have made for dangerous riding on windy days. This unusual scene is from the Borelli Collection in the archives of the Museum of Farnham.

Despite the obvious sunshine (including a man with a sunshade), there are only two people with bare heads in this picture – both competitors – in the rope climbing event at Broomleaf sports day. The poles on which the ropes are fixed must have been lashed together very well to prevent the cross-bar slipping while men were climbing.

PC Bill Stoves of Farnham Police Station organized an event in July 1987, to raise money for charity. It was the world's longest paper chain and gained for its organizer a spot on the television programme *Record Breakers*. The paper chain, some of which can be seen in Lower Church Lane, stretched right round the town and into Farnham Park on Sunday afternoon 12 July. It was photographed both from the ground and the air to make certain that it was one continuous chain without a break. Every paper link, each about fourteen inches long, was put together by hand.

It must have been a very important moment, when this photograph was taken, because the gentleman wearing the boater is a member of the Borelli family, outside whose shop in The Borough, everyone is standing and the shop door is open wide. Surely no Edwardian shopkeeper would behave in such a casual way unless it was for something particularly out-of-the-ordinary? The glass panel above the door, stating that Borelli's had the Royal Appointment as watchmakers to Queen Victoria, can still be seen today.

Despite the old-fashioned appearance of the people and what could be taken for a rural setting, this scene, in 1972, is one of the cast in *The Queen's Highland Servant* which was playing at the Castle Theatre. The site is that of one left by the recently demolished Rose's shop in East Street, and during the run of the play, from 18 April to 6 May, the cast took time out of the theatre to publicize the selling of bricks to help raise money for the new theatre, the Redgrave, which was to be completed two years later.

Above: During the summer of 1975, Waverley Borough Council ran its first free playscheme for local children. The Farnham sessions were held at the Memorial Hall under its leader, Jean Parratt, centre, who was assisted by members of her family — a necessary requirement because of 2,895 attendances over the twenty days (forty sessions) for which the scheme ran. Here, taking part in a dressing-up session are a few of those children who attended, including Verna Carey, Tracey Warren, Barry Lawrence and Janice Frizell.

Left: Crosby Doors, the door and window factory which once stood adjacent to the Memorial Ground, gave the children at the playscheme, above, a large wooden fort which had been used in a carnival. This was the stage for many plays and on the left Peter Wolverson, the eldest of three brothers who attended the sessions, is protecting his 'lady,' Heather David.

Above: When Arch Parratt, right, drank this pint of his father's home-made cider in 1925, before going off for a spin on his motor bike, neither he, nor his father, Arthur, had ever considered a time when there could be drink/drive laws. Parratt father and son are standing in their garden in the High Street, Rowledge, where Arthur had his home-made cider press. In the autumn, when the apples were being crushed and wasps swarmed round him, he would crush offending insects between his forefinger and thumb, a feat which astonished his grandson, Ted.

Right: Arch Parratt bought his first motor-bike, a Henley Blackburn, from the Heath Brothers of Frensham, who ran a motor-cycle business which began from a shed in their back garden. On 12 April 1920, when this licence was issued in Rowledge, Arch had to pay the full £1.0.0. annual fee, although the licence expired on 31 December, only eight months later.

Nº 152209

Licence for One Motor Bicycle or Tricycle at £1:0:0.

* _Archibald Arthur Parratt_

of _Jubilee ... Rowledge._ in the

Civil Parish or Township of _Farnham_ within the

Administrative County† _of_

is hereby authorized to keep ONE MOTOR BICYCLE or TRICYCLE, from the date hereof until the *31st day of December* next following: the sum of ONE POUND having been paid for this Licence.

Granted at _Rowledge_

this _12th_ day of _April_ 19 20

by _M. Gilbert._

* NOTE—Name to be inserted in full.
†If the residence is within a County Borough strike out "Administrative" and insert "Borough" after "County".
S.D. 1919.

41

When the Bourne Cricket Club held its annual dinner on 19 November 1971 the top table guests, as shown here, included at least three residents from Hale. Harry Lawrence, who was then Hale village's newsagent, left, can be seen chatting to Dorothy Cordier. Hale's postmistress and her husband, Frank, is on Dorothy's left. Both Harry Lawrence and Frank Cordier became local councillors.

These Farnham people are off for a charabanc ride in an Aldershot and District Traction Company (Traco) vehicle with a soft top, so that the passengers can enjoy the sun on the way to the coast. Few people had cars in those days and a trip such as this was the highlight of the year.

In this Edwardian scene there are several baby carriages, a number of children, a reasonable amount of bunting but not a single bare head to be seen. The venue for this event was Gostrey Meadow, on the occasion of its official opening. The Farnham Maltings can just be seen on the extreme left and the builder's merchant, Mardon & Mills, late Thompsett & Co., also advertised on its wall that it was a lime and cement merchant. Farnham's present police station is on the site today.

Just as in the picture above, this view of Farnham swimming baths when it opened in 1897, shows everyone wearing a hat – everyone that is, apart from the swimmer!

This is an interesting picture because all the staff of the Mariners Hotel at Millbridge, Frensham, are posing together. Each holds a tool of his or her trade; the lady on the extreme right wields her rolling pin. A rake, besom and mallet are among other items to be seen and the picture includes a small cask of beer. The photographer was most likely to have been Mr Sturt who also ran the post office and store at Millbridge.

A float from Nash's Bakery at Hale was decorated for one of Farnham's carnivals in the 1930s. The company's claim that its bread made children forget cake meant that it must have had a very high standard to maintain.

John Henry Knight, one of Farnham's best-known inventors and a photographer of exceptional skill, invented a wood spring tyre for use on the back wheels of cars, as can be seen above. A model of the spring can be seen in the Museum of Farnham. Despite the word 'spring', though, this low horse power vehicle is probably far more uncomfortable to be in then are the saddles of the one-horse power animals below, at Moor Park Riding Stables. The horses are being led by Edna Storey, who once lived in St. James's Avenue, opposite to the school which her children, John and Karen, attended.

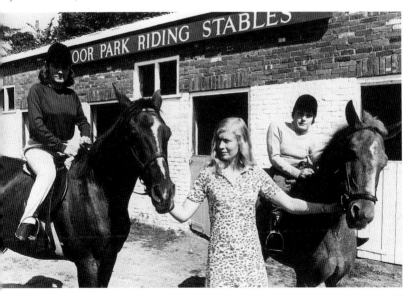

The young boy holding the reins of this horse and carriage is, despite his top hat, less than fourteen years old. The picture, taken just about a century ago, at Rowledge Post Office, shows Mr Porter's carriage and pair outside his shop in The Square. Judging by the items in the window and outside on the ground, the post office sold a variety of goods including tin baths and spades as well as postage stamps.

This time three horses are doing man's bidding, and are involved in ploughing fields at Badshot Lea for farm worker Henry Franks. This photograph is from Trevor Wells' *The Tinseys of Badshot Lea*, a history of his wife's family.

Farnham Horticultural Society had an outing during the 1930s, not to some faraway place such as Wisley but just down the road, two miles out of town, to Bide's nursery, at Runfold. The coach driver, left, wearing a white peaked cap and coat, was obviously invited to be photographed in addition to the society's members, whose day trip it was.

Percy Parratt and his wife, Dora, pose in their garden at Shortheath, with a cup which he had won for two of his prize dahlia blooms. Mr Parratt was renowned, throughout the area, for his dahlias which he exhibited at many village and town garden shows.

The same man appears in both of the pictures on this page. In The Lamb, above, Dick Burge is seen right, just before a darts match with 'Pike' Spencer. Mr Burge lived close to The Lamb, which was a Watney's public house for many years. In the picture below he is the clown, on the left, when the Jolly Boys Jazz Band, of which he was a member, were out raising funds in 1935, to build a new Trimmer's Hospital. The skeleton, in the centre, is Bill Young, a former licensee of the Black Prince, Hale, and who also worked in the gents' outfitting department of the Co-op in Union Road. Lilian Burge was the Dutch girl, Elsie Warilow (a baker) and 'Buddy' Fisher a chimney sweep.

The photograph above has not crept into a book about Farnham by mistake, despite part of Tower Bridge being visible in the background. The small boat in the foreground is the English *Rose lll* and Captain John Ridgway from Farnham, and his colleague, Chay Blyth, rowed up the River Thames, to Tower Pier, in 1966, to join a reception to launch their book, *A Fighting Chance*. Farnham journalist, on the *Surrey and Hants News*, David Johnstone, lost his life in the same challenge which Ridgway and Blyth had undertaken, to row the Atlantic.

The water at this drinking fountain in Gostrey Meadow quenched the thirst of children such as the niece and nephew of Evelyn 'Jo' Simmonds, a female photographer in this town, who took the picture with the children's mothers and grandmother. The fountain was to the design of Harold Falkner and in 1910, £21 for its cost was pledged by a Mr Patterson.

Above: Just mention the name of Annie Martin to almost anyone in Farnham who lived in the town between 1940 and 1980 and, inevitably, their eyes will light up and they will say: 'Dear old Annie.' She ran the greengrocery stall at the foot of Castle Street, for almost 40 years, helped by her son, John, and later by his children, too. John, known to many as 'Boy, Boy,' is on the right of this picture standing with a colleague. The grapes which can be seen in the centre of the stall are probably the Almeria variety, because, judging by the amount of clothing that the men are wearing, this picture must have been taken in winter in the late 1940s and this type of grape was the most easily available in those days, at that time of year.

Left: Annie Martin, a tiny woman, treated everyone the same, from Lord Montgomery of Alamein to the smallest child buying flowers for his or her mother on Mothering Sunday. She was interviewed by Brian Johnston for *Down Your Way* and, through this broadcast millions heard the Londoner's voice which was so well-known in Farnham, her adopted town, when she shouted, above the noise of the traffic, about the quality of the fruit and vegetables, (especially the strawberries), on her stall.

Five

Uniformed Brigades

Farnham men, women and children have been photographed in uniform from the earliest days of photography. Whether in war or peace there have always been plenty of opportunities to join organizations which are recognized by the special clothing that their members wear. One of Farnham's male photographers donned khaki in the Great War, and was blinded. The only woman photographer allowed to record the work of women in uniform in France and Flanders, in 1919, was Olive Edis, who also had a studio in Farnham. From choirboys to the bright blue uniforms of soldiers at the Shortheath Sanatorium, pictures of all can be found in this chapter.

With the exception of the upper part of the building in the centre almost everything else in this scene at the East Street/Bear Lane/Borough Junction has changed over the past sixty years snice this parade of choir and clergy took place at 5.35pm one spring evening. Hewitt & Lee were offering for sale the building which once housed the Fourteen Penny House; Alfred Wyles, draper and milliner, owned the prominent corner site; a large clock, over Sainsbury's grocery store, to the left of Wyles' shop, told the time and the signpost showing the way to Haslemere, Hindhead, Alton and Guildford, was constructed from wood.

Many large houses in the Farnham and Frensham areas were commandeered as hospitals during the First World War. The above picture was taken at Shortheath in 1917 and it would appear that there was almost one nurse for every soldier. Crutches and a wheelchair supply evidence of leg amputations and the nurses, many of whom were young girls from wealthy families who had not, until the outbreak of hostilities, even made their own beds let alone those of injured soldiers, must have found life very different from that in pre-war days. In the bottom picture, taken at the same sanatorium, the soldier in the back row, left, is holding a feather duster like a rifle, over his shoulder. The reason why is not known.

The incident in the picture above is very much a mystery. Several theories have been expounded but recently Mrs Dorothy Dimes, an octogenarian, said that she thought it was the funeral of a Countess who was foreign and died three days after giving birth to a son c. 1901. When the son died, aged 78, he was buried in the same vault in Farnham Cemetery as his mother. After research I discovered that a Countess Antoinette Seilern, from Austria, who died in 1901, aged 26 years, was buried in Farnham and her son, Count Antoine Edward Seilern, who died in 1978 was later buried beside her. On 16 September 1992 the lead-lined coffins of mother and son were exhumed and taken back to Austria. Mrs Dimes said that she had been told that 'half the population of Farnham' had turned out for the funeral of the Countess. 'And they wouldn't have walked that far along West Street unless it was something as special as that,' she ended. The number of uniformed gentlemen seems to signify it was a very special occasion.

Boy Scouts from Farnham, taken at Browndown Camp in August 1920. Humphrey Elphick is the boy at the back who is not wearing a hat.

Above: Forty-three burly policemen and one tiny boy were photographed outside the stables of the police station in Union Road, in the early 1920s. The child, Arthur Slaught, was the grandson of Supt. A. Simmonds, eighth from left, and he is seen wearing his late father's medal- the latter was killed the day before the armistice in the First World War – and the policemen adopted little Arthur as their mascot.

Left: When Irene Moulsley was fourteen years old, she went into service with the Kingham family, who owned a large grocery shop in West Street. That firm used horse-drawn carts to deliver some of their goods and Irene's father, a blacksmith in Upper Church Lane, probably helped shoe the animals, when necessary. Here Irene (now better known as Mrs Rene Conley), is wearing her housemaid's uniform.

Above: This group of ARP wardens were at their headquarters in Bridgefield, in 1942, when they took out their rope, hose, rattles, bell and two buckets to pose for the photographer. They are the Bridgefield, Fairfield and Darvill's Lane Section, Sector 18A, and are, back, left to right ?, Will Wisbey, ? Weeks, ? Willis, ? Reeves. Front row, left to right: ? Crowhurst, ? Ogbourne, ? Scott, ? Hale, ? Wyles. The group is sitting in the garden of Mr Scott's house, which doubled as their HQ and it looks as though a temporary wall has been built for protection around one of the windows of the house.

Right: Although looking somewhat informal Hilda Moulsley (now Ackroyd) is nevertheless in the turban, bib and brace uniform supplied to workers at Crosby Doors, West Street, where munitions were made during the Second World War. Hilda is sister to Irene the housemaid on the facing page.

Uniformed police and a detachment of firemen in their brass helmets, are in this procession which is en route to the cemetery in West Street. The bay window on the left is part of The Jolly Sailor public house and in 1842 there was a beer house on the site of the part-timbered building on the right. Known as the White Horse it was offered for sale in 1883 by Farnham Brewery and soon afterwards it was destroyed by fire.

On 14 August 1936 there was a gala performance of *Show Boat* at the Regal Cinema in East Street. Distinguished guests included HRH Lady Patricia Ramsay and General Sir Cecil Romer. The entire proceeds of the event were given to the Red Cross, some of whose members are on parade here.

At least seven drums can be seen being carried by this troop of First World War soldiers who were captured on film at Millbridge, Frensham, by Mr Sturt, who ran the village store and post office just a few yards from the point that the soldiers had reached.

Drums appear in this picture of men in uniform, too, but after the seven above, provided by the Army, here the Frensham Institute Band can only manage five. Even that number, though, is no mean feat for a small village contingent, the rest of whose musicians appear to play the fife.

Although much faded with the passing years, this photograph of the Farnham Fire Brigade, outside Broomleaf Farm, Waverley Lane, is interesting because of the way the service was run nearly a century ago. The fireman in the centre is Bill Brewer, an ostler at the Bush Hotel as well as a part-time fireman. When a fire alarm was sounded Bill had to get the horses together at the Bush Hotel and then rush up South Street to get them to where the fire wagon was kept at Broomleaf, over 500 yards away!

This picture of firemen, mostly wearing flat caps, is from the Borelli Collection and was taken in East Street c. 1896. Firemen pictured include: John and James Hawkes, Harry Patrick, Alf Bailey, Tom Hudson, Harry Luffry, Albert Budd, Chris Harrison, William Dalton, George Swan, John Chitty, Ernest Edwards, George Elliott, George Windibank, 'Shoey' Varnes, Capt. Elliott.

Above: The Farnham Boys' Brigade is seen here just before the outbreak of the Second World War, outside the Methodist Church in South Street. Included in this picture are Mrs Mayhew, Miss Tigwell (both uniformed leaders), Victor Burge, Eric Painter, Eric Blunden, Cecil Morgan, Maurice Sturt, Peter Blunden, Michael Hayter, David Gudgin, Alec Allen, John Bertie, Malcolm Payne, Stan Knotts and Pat Mulheron who later became a good friend of the Aldershot-born actor and comedian, Arthur English, the best-known 'spiv' in the country, who died in April 1995.

Right: Miss Tigwell, pictured in the third row from the front and second from the left, in the photograph above, ran a toy shop in South Street which was a mecca for small children — even if they could only gaze in the windows through lack of money to make a purchase. Her tiny, green-painted shop stood in a row with other small businesses but all were demolished in the late 1970s to make way for Farnham's third Sainsbury store.

Above: Eugene Fuller, who owned the Delaunay Studio in West Street, was sent white feathers in the early part of the First World War, suggesting that he was a coward. He therefore joined the Army, leaving his studio in the hands of Evelyn 'Jo' Simmonds, a daughter of the Police Superintendent. Soon after Eugene drew this picture of a tank and men in a bunker in France, in 1917, he was blinded and Miss Simmonds continued to run the studio alone from then onwards, Farnham's only permanent female photographer at that time.

Left: Evelyn 'Jo' Simmonds, taken when she was in her mid-eighties, at her home in Firgrove Hill. She never married because her fiancé, John Wells, was killed in a motorcycle accident three weeks before the arranged wedding day. She was an excellent photographer, a good letter-writer and a reliable friend to many people of both sexes.

Men of 5 Platoon 'A' Coy. 2nd Surrey Bn. Home Guard, December 1944. pictured outside the main door of Farnham Grammar School where some of them were teachers. Back row, left to right: Private P.H. Mills, Pte. A. G. Brown, Pte. C. Richards, Lance Corporal G.A. Puttick, Pte. F.A. Holloway, Pte. A.C. Hunt, Pte. D.St.G. Clarke. Second row: Pte. F.G. Kemp, Pte. S.H. Tubb, Pte. C.G.Tucker, Pte. W.E. Hawkins, Pte. R.T. Saunders, Pte. C.G. Hacon, Pte. J.E. Young, Pte. G. Noble. Third row: Pte. C. Ralph, Pte. R.C. Johns, L/Cpl. C.J. Broadhurst, Pte. S.L. Jones, L/Cpl. L.V. Lance, L/Cpl. H. Beeken, Pte. M. Kennedy, Pte. H.H. Williams, Pte. T.P. Cannon. Fourth row: Pte. A.G. Goddard, Pte. C.O. Hofvander, Pte. L. Byrne, Pte. W.A. Smallman, Pte. E.J. Lickfold, Pte. C.E. Hatcher, L/Cpl. N.A. Barter, Pte. E.F. Baker, Pte. R.S. Shrubb, Pte. E.A .Goddard, Pte. J.E. Goddard, Pte. S.F. Horwill, Pte. F.. Mileham, L/Cpl. R.B. Varey. Front row: Corporal S.M. Lamport, Cpl. F. Brown, Cpl. J.H. Spedding, Sergeant E.R. Usherwood, Sgt. G. Gardiner, Lieutenant S.E. Lock, Lt. F.A. Morgan M.C. (headmaster of Farnham Grammar School), Sgt. R. Grimes, Sgt. S.D. Horner, Sgt. H.C. Montagu, Cpl. G.H. Ridout, Cpl. E.W. Godsil, Cpl. W.F. Burge. This photograph was taken by Gale and Polden, Aldershot, at one time the printers and publishers of the Aldershot News series which had a large printing works opposite to the Aldershot Bus Station. One of Pte. Hawkins' daughters remembers her father having a long day at work and then rushing home, putting on his Home Guard uniform and hurrying up into Farnham Park for drill – 'and he was over sixty, then,' she said, 'we thought it was too much for him.'

Olive Edis was born in 1876 and took up photography as a career in 1900, having a studio in Norfolk and in Castle Street, Farnham. The advertisement on this page announces the photographer's arrival in town for her regular, annual four-month season here. In 1914 she was accepted as a member of the Royal Photographic Society. Towards the end of the First World War she was commissioned by the Women's Work Committee of the Imperial War Museum, to travel to France and Flanders and to record, on photographic plate, the work done by British women who were nursing the wounded and helping in many other ways. It took over nine months of frustrating organization to set up this tour so it did not begin until March 1919, when the war had ended, but there was still much for Olive, the only female photographer to be given permission to photograph in the war zone, to record. All of her work is of exceptional quality and some of it is held in the National Portrait Gallery. Other photographs are in the possession of members of her family one of whom gave permission for the self-portrait, on the left, to be included in this volume.

These soldiers are lined up in Farnham Park during the First World War. When the photograph is inspected closely it is interesting to see that almost every man is smiling and looking happy about going off to serve King and Country. The officer in the front has a uniform which is of much better material than those worn by the men. Whereas his is smooth, once his belt is fastened, the men's jackets appear crumpled. What appears to be a slatted periscope behind the men is, in fact, a casing to protect a tree.

Only one doctor in the group of six above treated patients for the entire lifetime of Trimmer's Hospital at its Menin Way location. That one was Dr Town Jones, third from left. Matron is the only person who wears uniform and she looks very severe even though, according to the wife of a doctor not pictured, she was 'absolutely super.' Her name was Miss Brammer and she came from Yorkshire. From left to right the other doctors are: Dr Halliwell, Dr Pemberley, Dr Roberts, Dr Hobbs and Dr Caldecott.

A wartime cartoon drawn by Marshall Barnes and published in a newspaper, shows the chaos caused to men in uniform who did not know the area they were in and found street signs either removed or altered, so that the enemy would not have an advantage should they invade these shores. This is Bridge Square, although the sign at Firgrove Hill indicates that as being the route to Guildford.

In the 1920s there was a song in which the words ran: 'Here comes the Boys' Brigade, All covered in marmalade, A twopenny pillbox on their heads And a half-a-yard of braid.' There are plenty of pillbox hats in this picture taken outside the Methodist Church Hall, South Street, c. 1958. Jack Mayhew is standing extreme right.

Six

Going Up, Coming Down

"Now, what was on that site?" is a question frequently heard from people who return to Farnham after many years. To many people too much of the main part of Farnham has been lost to developers over the past couple of decades – East Street, part of which became The Woolmead, in particular. In this section, therefore, there is a chance to see, once again, the comings and goings of some familiar landmarks in the town.

When the Regal Cinema (latterly known as Studios One and Two) suddenly closed in 1985, many people were angry but, they thought, it will re-open again, surely? However, it did not have a new lease of life and in this picture, taken from the rear of the cinema where the screen had once stood, many thousands of small, red bricks, made in Farnham, are seen having been broken out from the wall and dropped on to the ground. A few people retrieved mementoes of happy times spent within the cinema's dark interior, including one lady who begged from the demolition workers (and achieved her objective) an iron and plush tip-up seat from the back row of the stalls.

The two pictures on this page were taken from almost the same position (note the house with the tall chimney on the left). The upper view shows Mills & Sons removing some large pieces of stone from Castle Street demolition work c. 1929 and surely the horsedrawn cart must be blocking the traffic? In the lower picture it would seem that rain stopped work on the demolition of the Town Hall Building. Both pictures on this page are from the Borelli Collection in the archives of the Museum of Farnham.

Above: The notice at the side of this picture reads: 'Nothing but the truth,' but the truth in this case could be questioned somewhat. The building being reconstructed, by Crosby Doors, now gives the impression of great antiquity, hardly the truth when it was only rebuilt in 1922 or thereabouts!

Right: In the early 1920s the Spinning Wheel, formerly the second site of The Goat's Head, was renovated. It is interesting to note that the scaffolding poles are set in wooden barrels, presumably with something heavy like cement inside them. The beams on this building remain those which were originally used in the seventeenth century, but, as the building in the picture above is the same as that on the right of this one, it is easily seen that however old the present 'Next' fascia looks, it is really only of twentieth-century origin.

It is almost 2,000 years since these pieces of stone were put together to make a Roman bath house. The remains of the walls which were built around 116AD at a site close to the present Six Bells public house, are still in position but under eighteen inches of earth. At one time Farnham Urban District Council had intended to put a roof over the ruins so that the public could view them, but this came to nought. This photograph was taken soon after the discovery of a Roman bath and villa when the post-war housing estate was being constructed in 1946/7. The estate was named after the finds and is known as Roman Way today.

Proof, if ever any was needed that the frontage of Lion and Lamb Yard is of twentieth-century origin, can be seen in this picture in the Borelli Collection. It was taken in the 1920s, when the present building, adjacent to the Farnham Herald offices, was being rebuilt.

Both of the photographs on this page are from the Borelli Collection in the Museum of Farnham. The view above is in The Borough, when the old Town Hall was being demolished. The building on the extreme right is the present W.H.Smith shop, which has been at the same site since 1935. Mills & Sons were the builders and the half-demolished semi-circular structure was once known as the Corn Exchange. A tyre is used as a ten mph speed limit sign on the lamp-post at the junction of Castle Street and The Borough (below) seen before the rebuilding of the Town Hall Buildings. The man in the dark coat, centre, is standing at what is approximately the site of Martin's fruit and vegetable stall.

It is almost seventy years since the man in the left-hand picture stood on the top of the tower of the old Town Hall building and carefully took down the wooden structure, plank by plank. On the right is the building just after demolition began. A large archway entrance faces the former Hale's radio shop and a sign for Frisby's, where shoes and boots were sold for over 80 years, is in the foreground beneath a street lamp.

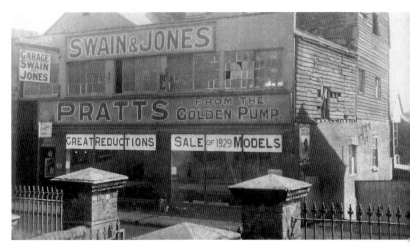

There were great reductions on the prices of 1929 cars at Swain and Jones, East Street, when demolition work was being carried out on the roof of the garage. The pillars in the foreground formed the entrance to the old knitting factory.

It is not clear from this photograph c. 1929, whether the Assembly Rooms in South Street were being demolished or just painted, but as in earlier pictures beer barrels have been used as the base for the scaffolding poles. Concerts were held in this building and it was also where "Boy" McCormick, the town's famous boxer in the 1920s, used to spar.

Although this building, in South Street, was less than 100 years old when it was knocked down, the attractive roofs over the bay windows were a loss to the street scene. South Street, originally known as New Road, was constructed in 1868, at a total cost of £2,312 10s 0d. The trees in the distance are in Gostrey Meadow. The tall building, Expedier House, was demolished in the 1980s.

A Mayor of Waverley, Anne Hoath, is seen re-burying a time capsule before work began on the construction of the supermarket and car park in The Hart. The store replaced William Kingham's wholesale grocery warehouse – which had contained the same time capsule placed in its foundation stone in September 1953 – and in the background Mr Michael F.P. Kingham, a great-grandson of the grocery firm's founder, is watching with interest. When the warehouse was empty, the capsule which had been in a cavity at the front of the building, was stolen but, after an appeal Mr Andrew Sturt, left, the managing director of Arundell House Securities, one of the developers responsible for The Hart/Lion and Lamb complex had it returned anonymously. The building in the background is the Farnham Baptist Church.

Seven

Hopping Mad

It would be almost impossible to consider a book about Farnham which did not include at least a mention of hops, brewing and public houses. The town which at one time was reputed to have more hostelries per head of population than any other town in the country had its hopping, drinking, heyday century between 1850 and 1950. Today, although the number of pubs has declined the choice of beers is still extensive with real ale brews from many parts of the country and from mini-breweries as well as the Big Seven. Add to these points the annual Beerex at Farnham Maltings and the words of Farnham and beer remain inextricably entwined in many people's minds.

This mock-Tudor building at the top of Downing Street was formerly owned by the Farnham United Breweries but it was taken over by Courage and Company in a massive sale of pubs in 1927. It dispensed beer from about 1860 when it was owned by George Trimmer, one of the town's great benefactors. The Alliance was rebuilt in the 1930s to the design of G. Maxwell Aylwin and Harold Falkner, but before this took place there was access at the rear of the building above, from where 'ladies of ill-repute' were said to operate.

All three pictures on this page are buildings where beer was once dispensed. Top left is the former Greyhound, in Hale Road which faced the Farnham Workhouse. Top right is the building which was known as The Surrey Arms, in East Street. It was closed down by the Farnham Magistrates in June 1921. On the left the former Fourteen Penny House can be seen. It was in the building which has a Lyons Tea sign on its side wall. The view is from the first Cambridge Place, looking across East Street. After the demolition of the butcher's shop (closest to the camera lens) and other shops at this end of East Street, the name of Cambridge Place was given to the pedestrian entrance to the third site of a Sainsbury store in Farnham.

The Marlborough Head and Seven Stars, in East Street, today both look, at first glance, to be picturesque Tudor buildings. The picture above shows the former building, before it was rebuilt in 1929/30, when the architect was John Howard of Haslemere and the builders were Mardon and Mills of Farnham. On the left is The Grotto, a shop which was much-loved by children who had farthings to spend on sweets. The owner's husband was crippled and it is probably he who is sitting outside the shop watching the children enter. Crowley & Co., from Alton, supplied beer to the Marlborough Head while that at the Seven Stars, below, came from the Farnham United Breweries Ltd. The building on the right has not changed at all and, today, houses H.C. Patrick, undertaker. Both photographs on this page are from the Borelli Collection.

Few people who go to the large motel on the A325 at Holt Pound today could possibly imagine that in the centre of the complex are the walls of the building seen above. The Forest Inn, about two miles from Farnham town centre, once had carts and horses where cars now pull in and the grassed area to the rear was the cricket ground known as The Oval, where Billy Beldham, one of this country's great cricketers, played. This pub also sported a cricket team with every player bearing the local surname of Parratt.

This crowd is outside The Lamb, Abbey Street, in the late 1920s. Mr Benwell is on the extreme right and Dick Burge is seventh from the right. The Lamb was then under the Watney livery.

Although none of the names of the people in these pictures is known they have been included in the Hopping Mad section because of their clothing when out in hop gardens. The news that a photographer was to capture them on glass plate negatives must have been given in advance for the superb turn-out of clothing to be worn in a working environment. The small girl in the centre of the top picture is probably the 'Hop Queen' in her particular garden and, possibly the tiny girl in an unusual bonnet, fills the same rôle in the lower picture. A hop-puller, with his pole, is second left, in the top picture which was taken in The Hart hop gardens.

These pictures could be joined by the words 'the beginning and the end.' The top view is from the hop gardens at the top of Castle Street, with the road leading to Folly Hill looking like a cart track on the left. The hops are growing on poles, not on strings as in later years. A farm cart, piled with hay, can just be seen in the distance. In the lower picture the hop bines have been taken into large sheds, at Badshot Lea, for the hop cones to be picked mechanically rather than in the time-honoured fashion, by hand, as the families were doing on the previous page.

Despite the frequency at which this view across Longbridge is seen, it is always possible to find a different picture. In this view the angles at which the words Free House are set on both sides of the centre, first floor window, are what makes for its unusual detail. Here at the Jolly Farmer, William Cobbett was born in 1763. He was an author, journalist and radical politician, yet he never went to school - his family could not pay the fees, so he taught himself. He was the founder of *Hansard*, the record of the proceedings of the House of Commons each day.

Although badly damaged this rare picture, dated 1926, gives details of the Queen Street Tavern where mine host was William Stone. The float in the centre is decorated to look like the pub, at the corner of Bear Lane, but which was more commonly called the Fourteen Penny House, where Barrett's noted Farnham ales were sold. The front float represents the Market Hall, which once stood at the bottom of Castle Street.

Above: The only clue to where this rare photograph was taken is the railway signal which can be seen slightly to the left of the building. Two oast houses, in which hops were dried, are easily identifiable and the building is part of Broomleaf Farm, and stands diagonally opposite to Farnham Station.

Left: Thomas Mathews, brewer of ale, stout, porter and pale ale produced his beers at the Lion and Lamb Brewery, West Street. In 1890 he won two medals at the Brewers' Exhibition in London. The Museum of Farnham has one or two (empty) beer bottles from both Mathews' Brewery and Farnham United Breweries, on display.

Above: There was a public house on this site for at least 225 years, until the early 1990s when the building above was demolished, following a murder which took place outside. During the 1980s the Watney Brewery tried altering its image by making a number of its pubs take on the Phoenix livery, which can be seen on the sign and on the wall lights. Other names for 'watering holes' on this site have been the Adam and Eve, the King of Prussia, the Pocket of Hops and the Downing Street Club. It is said that ghostly screams and rumbling carriage wheels emanate from the ghosts at this spot.

Right: Under its extended name of Watney, Combe and Reid, Watneys once had a brewery in Castle Street which, in 1891, was put up for auction, together with a number of pubs. The name can still be read on marks in the wood across the archway, now with St Georges Yard on it, which led into the site. The auctioneer, Mr J. Alfred Eggar, owned the property to the right of the archway.

Plan of
OLD ESTABLISHED
FREEHOLD BREWERY
SITUATE IN
Castle Street, Farnham, Surrey.
AND
THIRTEEN FULLY LICENSED HOUSES
SITUATE IN
FARNHAM, CRONDALL, ALTON, & MEDSTEAD.
ALSO
Four fully licensed Leasehold Houses.
SITUATED IN NEIGHBOURHOOD OF
FARNHAM, UPPER HALE & BENTWORTH.
For Sale by Auction by
MR J. ALFRED EGGAR
at the BUSH HOTEL, FARNHAM.
ON TUESDAY JUNE 23RD 1891.
AT THREE O'CLOCK PRECISELY.

The pub sign on the extreme left is that of the Bell and Crown, a hostelry known by that name from 1799. This is a very early photograph of Castle Street, hence its muddy appearance. The Market House, built in 1568, is modelled in the carnival float picture on page 79. This building was demolished in 1863 and the discarded timbers were used in a new house on East Street. This in turn was renovated in 1994 and the old timbers were thown on a skip but rescued by Chris Hellier, who was then a volunteer worker at the Museum of Farnham. They are now being used again – in a building at the Rural Life Centre Museum, Tilford.

The Cherry Tree public house, Rowledge, c. 1920, with a sign on the wall stating that dinners and teas were provided. In the 1890s, under a Mr Rogers, it served three functions – it was a baker's, grocer's and an inn.

Eight

The Inside Story

In the days before flashlights, photography inside buildings was not an easy matter. It was not until the 1950s that the amateur, with luck, could get reasonable prints. The professional portrait photographer, of course, had his cameras in studio conditions but the equipment was so cumbersome that it was not easy to take it out on location. This means, therefore, that inside views of buildings are rare until after the end of the Second World War.

Downing Street once had as many as five fish shops at one time. One owner was Charlie Barnes, second from right, serving a pair of kippers from his cold slab in 1962. He advertised himself as a high class fishmonger and poulterer, a dealer in game and all frozen foods. Unusually for the early 1960s, he also sold barbecued chicken as a speciality.

On Monday 5 August 1985 Margaret Thatcher, who was the Prime Minister of the day, paid a visit to the head office of Farnham Castle Newspapers in West Street, at the invitation of the owner, Ray Tindle. She was photographed both outside the building and in the print room with many of the staff of the day around her. The newspaper, which can be seen on the machine, left, was the *Surrey and Hants News*, Surrey's oldest newspaper, and Mr Tindle invited the Prime Minister to start the machinery to print it. As the first newspapers came off the press Mrs Thatcher saw herself on the front in a photograph which had been taken in the street only minutes earlier. She was also given a tour of the *Farnham Herald* offices to the front and above the print room. In addition to Mr Tindle, who was knighted in 1994 and who is standing next to the Prime Minister, Mr Tindle's wife, Beryl, is on the extreme right. Alan Smallman and Kevin Cruden, Mayors of Farnham and Waverley respectively are in the front row as is Dennis Stone, Reg Hatt (a former *Herald* editor) and Harold Cole (who worked on the *Farnham Herald* for 64 years). Among others are Robin Radley and Guy Bellamy, then editors of the *Herald* series and *Surrey and Hants News* series respectively, Angela Needs, Martyn Harris, Bob Doran, Diana Rosignoli, Charlie Hawkins, Brian Smallbone, Peggy Chapman, Alex Tait, Pam Crow, George Sallis, Betty Futcher, Jean Parratt, Cliff Morris and Colin Christmas. This picture, taken by a staff photographer, appeared in the *Farnham Herald* on the Friday after Mrs Thatcher's visit.

The children in the co-educational Frensham Heights School, at Rowledge, above, look more relaxed than in any school photograph I have seen of the pre-Second World War period. This room had been part of Frensham Hill Hospital in the First World War. Before that it was owned by a Mr Charrington, owner of the national brewery concern. The lower interior shot is far less happy. The photograph was taken on the day after the last pupils attended what had hitherto been an excellent primary and first school known first as East Street and later as The Park School. Dwindling pupil numbers forced its closure and the building is now a centre for the social services.

For almost 100 years Crosby's operated from various sites in Farnham. Their most famous location, though, was at the western end of town where, during the Second World War, they made munitions boxes and other vital items for the war effort. After the war the firm concentrated on doors and windows. Now nothing is left of Crosby's. It was reduced to rubble and is under the new estate of homes, offices and workshop units adjacent to the Memorial Hall. The picture above shows part of the factory when it was in full door production.

In these days of unisex hairdressers where customers sit in the window to have a perm or short-back-and-sides, the idea of each lady being ensconced in a private cubicle with an oak-panelled door, as in the sketch above, seems most bizarre. This interior view of Lionel Smith's, the hairdresser who operated from 1 The Borough, was drawn c. 1935.

Although it might seem strange, there is a religious connection between these two interior views. In the upper scene the sunshine streams through the window of Farnham Castle's chapel in this postcard produced by Frith and Company c. 1910. All the lighting in the chapel was by candlelight so the photographer made good use of the natural light for this picture. Below, an aluminium kettle and black telephone are the only artefacts remaining in what had once been a meeting hall and library at Alma Lane, Heath End. Against the wishes of many local people, the Rev. Michael Sellors, Vicar of Hale, sold the building, which was demolished and a house was built in its place, almost opposite to the Alma Way entrance. The hall had been church property so St John's and St Mark's Churches gained from the sale.

The bacon department at Kingham's wholesale unit in The Hart looks clean and bright. This picture is taken from Kingham's booklet which was produced to launch the warehouse. It includes details of what had been placed in the time capsule mentioned elsewhere in this book. The objects included a set each of 1953 Coronation coins and stamps, current copies of *The Grocer* magazine and the *Daily Telegraph*, corn and hops.

Few books have glimpses inside tiled public toilets but this building is important. Number 1 Park Row, a cottage with four bedrooms, was altered into toilets in 1932, for the convenience of coach passengers who alighted in Castle Street and, in time it vied with the castle as being Farnham's most important tourist attraction, according to Bill Ewbank Smith in *Farnham In War And Peace*. It was converted to offices in the mid-1980s, coaches no longer stopping in Castle Street!

Nine

Plying Their Trades

Many people believe that supermarkets and out-of-town stores are killing the business of the small traders in Farnham. It is true that many of the firms which have traded here for decades, such as Hale's radio shop and Silver's, the gentlemen's outfitters, which between them notched up almost 150 years in the town, closed within six months of each other in the winter of 1994/5. It is therefore important to record the small firms of the past for historians of the future.

It seems impossible today to imagine this scene at a spot just a few yards from the continuous roar of traffic on the A31 in the building which is, in 1995, used as the Redgrave Theatre costume store. This is another of the photographs from the Borelli Collection and shows Samuel Bide's Hatch Mill Dairy, complete with a milk churn on a horse-drawn cart and the only person who appears to be working, one milkmaid carrying two buckets. The six men and one youth seem content to down tools and pose for the photographer.

The idea of a butcher having all his meat open to the fumes and dust of the street would be unthinkable today but here, George Hawkins stands proudly by the shoulders of lamb which hang from hooks in the open air. His shop, which had shutters pulled down at night, rather than panes of glass as is customary today, was on the corner of the first Cambridge Place, off East Street. Part of the wall of the Royal Deer can just be seen on the right.

E. Kimber ran a fruiterer and florist's shop in Castle Street, next door to the Coach and Horses. The archway to the right can still be seen today and is the present entrance to another trade of the past, a pawnbroker. Kimber's slogan was: 'We serve ourselves best by serving others better.' In 1934 fire gutted the store at the back of this shop.

The wife of Alan Bateman, the owner of the Farnham Motor Company in East Street, seen above, made the headlines in 1926 when she rescued a twenty-two-month-old baby from the River Wey in Gostrey Meadow. The child, Renee Smith, had been attracted by the ducks, it was believed, and dogs were being attracted by them, too. Accordingly the council ordered its surveyor to have the number of ducks reduced to eight.

The Reid's Stout sign on the wall shows where the entrance to the Watney, Combe and Reid depot was in Castle Street. Weller Eggar, estate agent and auctioneers, is in the background and Bill Brewer from Abbey Street is observing the ladies at a bric-a-brac stall. The site of the stall is also the place where the first two-minute silence, in memory of those who fell in the First World War, was held in 1916.

William Kingham and Sons' retail grocery shop was at 16, 17 and 18 West Street, adjacent to Church Passage. Bacon was cured at the back of the building giving rise to the nickname of the passage which lead to the church, as well as going down the side of the wall of the smoking area. The ironstone sets in this passage were in strips of different sized stones giving the appearance of a rasher of fatty bacon, hence the footpath became known as Streaky Bacon Lane. Sponges, of the deep sea variety, fill this window of the grocery shop, presumably for a special promotion. For over a century Farnham residents shopped at Kingham's, which later had branches at Reading and Chippenham as well as in Farnham.

Walter Moulsley, blacksmith, outside the forge in Upper Church Lane, with his sons, Walter, Eric and Leonard c.1930. On the left is part of the wall of the old Baker's Arms.

Williamson's, in The Borough, almost facing the Queen's Head, sold an assortment of products in the first decade of the twentieth century. It may have been because it was owned by two maiden ladies that Berlin Wools featured strongly in the advertising. The shop was an agent for Raphael Tuck post cards (two words as opposed to our present one), and the ladies also acted in the capacity of a news agent (also two words then). The board outside gives information on the latest news in the *Daily Mail* – the Montagu Court Martial.

Few, if any people who walk into Seven's Wine Bar today realize that they are going to eat and drink in a place which stands next door to the building where 'Triticumina Bread as supplied to her Majesty The Queen' was dispensed about 80 years ago. The first floor dining area of the present restaurant once bore many advertisements for the products sold in that building's interior when it was known as Barrett's Stores – turpentine, linseed oil, baths, pails, lamp glasses and wicks amongst them. Veritas mantles were also available. A choice of shoe polish was on offer in this stretch of The Borough. Barrett's stocked Jackson's Boot Polish whereas on the shop window, extreme left, the public is being exhorted to use Nugget Polishes.

The name of this company is displayed on the roof of the building on the right. The greenhouses are all part of Bide's Nursery in 1925. The photograph was taken by Dick Bide. The Aldershot gasholder can just be seen on the horizon. This has been retained as an item of industrial historic interest, unlike its Farnham counterpart, which was demolished.

Peter Broom, a Farnham councillor, was left-handed. He had such difficulty in finding equipment for people with a similar condition to himself that he opened a shop in London, in 1969, and customers went to it from all over the world. He was killed in a road accident in 1987. Before her marriage in 1929, Winifred Farr worked for four years in one of Farnham's lesser-known businesses, The Weavers, in Lion and Lamb Yard. The owner was Arthur Herring and he had a good trade from American tourists as well as from London stores.

In the Edwardian period Mr Hawgood, who was a 'Dealer in Old China Curios' as well as a house furnisher, had a large shop in East Street which was bounded on one side by Mrs Winslade who ran the Green Man and on the other by E. Lawrence, mine host at the Unicorn. Hawgood's shop was situated approximately where Peacocks is today.

The building on the left was demolished in the late 1980s to make way for a new office and housing development by Allamanda Estates and Kents Developments. Ken Kent bought the title of Lord of the Manor of Farnham at about the same time. Throughout the Second World War the Drill Hall, as this building was known, was a meeting place for the Home Guard. During its final years it was a licensed club known as Yogi's, also the Buckingham Snooker and Social Club. Karim Lawji, one of the snooker club's owners, came to England with his parents, brother Shamsher and sister Tamsin, in the early 1970s, to escape the Idi Amin régime in Uganda.

The Borough c. 1920, with the *Surrey and Hants News'* first office on the left, where delivery boys are chatting. J.E. Spencer silk mercer and fancy draper is on the right and other businesses which can be glimpsed include Usher's, where Michelin tyres could be purchased, Tigwell's the newsagent, who later moved to South Street, John Farmer's boot store, Barrett's ironmonger's, Sturt's stationers and Timothy Whites the chemist.

East Street c 1920, was a relatively quiet place, despite the presence of two cars in the street. Hawkins the butcher's, right, is distinguished by its carved name board. Wasley, fishmonger and poulterer can be seen, left, as well as the Farnham Cycle Works. The shop with white blinds outside is James Smyth, which opened before the First World War. It occupied the building which had earlier been Farnham High School for Girls.

R. Lorriman's leather shop is on the corner of Upper Church Lane with the Parish Church in the background. Two cottages occupied the spot which now has two shops and the gateway beyond them led to the back of Worsam's the bakery, where bread was kneaded for over 200 years.

This photograph was taken c. 1939 judging by the criss-cross of paper on the windows of Davies' newsagent's. Wasley's fishmonger, (see previous page), had closed down and to date no new tenant had been found although the white enamelled signs for Fry's chocolate can still be seen on the windows of G. Pomfret's confectioners. Pomfret's later moved along East Street, closer to the Seven Stars. Parking cars on the pavement was evidently allowed at the time!

For those people who had travelled down from London on the steam trains during 1933, the sight of the Station Hill tearooms, next to the level crossing, must have been a welcome one as they alighted on to the platform. A sign for Fenn's Mineral Waters (made in West Street) indicates that drinks other than tea were available and passers-by were invited to telephone from the tearoom if they wished.

The building in the centre is one which has been rebuilt at least three times in the twentieth century. It is The Alliance public house at the top of Downing Street, and this picture, although faded, is interesting because it has seldom been seen before. The fascia states that the building is a wholesale and retail outlet for wines and spirits. At the time this photograph was taken the property belonged to George Trimmer, a prosperous brewer, who died in 1892.

The Co-op in Union Road, as it appeared in 1962, with traffic passing in both directions can be seen above. Bill Young, who appears in one of the Jolly Jazz Boys photographs in this book, was the manager of the central part of this shop, the gentlemen's outfitting department. This was also the part of the building which, when still a shop, had once been a chapel and which still had the words of the Lord's Prayer on the wall above the cash desk – albeit the text was covered over with emulsion paint.

A view of East Street in 1962, before all these buildings were demolished to make way for The Woolmead. Heath Bros., the cycle shop, was the successor to the Farnham Cycle Company, seen in two earlier pictures in this section.

Ten

The More We Are Together...

...the merrier we shall be," say the words of a popular song of the 1930s and there have been many occasions in Farnham's history when groups of people have met, to sing, act, dance, play games or raise money for good causes. In this section events of this type are recorded as well as the participants, though some are disguised beyond recognition, even by their families.

This cheerful group of young ladies were all members of the Methodist Youth Club c. 1960. In addition to Pam and Joan Dare, who are unmistakable as twin sisters, other girls included are Bernadine Bowdery, Moira Hutchinson, Jennifer Collins, Sally Poulter, Margaret Edwards, Elizabeth Birch, and Margaret Bowdery. The photograph was taken by Mr J. Sargeant who lived in The Fairfield, a man who recorded most of the events which took place at the Methodist Church Hall as well as the weddings of members of that church.

Canon Crum, a much-respected Rector of Farnham Parish Church, is sitting in the centre of this group of choristers. When the Rev. Crum left the town on Monday 17 September 1928, he chose, as a leaving present from the parish, what was described by Bill Ewbank Smith in his book *Farnham in War and Peace* as one of the new 'toys of civilization,' a wireless receiving set. In thanking the parishioners, the Canon mentioned that he could claim a family connection with the science of sound transmission through his Uncle William – Lord Kelvin, 1824-1907 – who had laid the first cable across the Atlantic. Mr Ewbank Smith continued: 'Privately-owned wireless sets were gradually finding their way into people's homes. Mrs Philip Snowden of Eden Lodge, Tilford, told an audience in October that she looked forward to the time when sets were as common in houses as baths.' In the back row of this choral line-up are: Mr Elphick, Mr Dale, Mr Lee, Mr Chuter. Other singers include: Messrs Tomlin, Winslade, Figg, King, Vigar, Garman, Warren, Osborne, German, Hester, Carter, Pullen. Boys include: Teddy Warren, Jack Wing, Kim Warren, Frank German, George Acock, Ted Marlow, Steve Stewart and ? Fosbury.

Farnham Jolly Boys Jazz Band raised a substantial sum for the Trimmer's Cottage Hospital Appeal c.1935 with their carnival entry, two photographs of which can be seen here. The pictures were taken outside Brightwell's Clinic, earlier this was Lowlands, a house owned by the Paget family, when a frequent visitor to it was Florence Nightingale. In the 1970s this building became part of the Redgrave Theatre. Included in fancy dress outfits are: Vera Weinmann, Lillian Weinmann, Dick Burge, Lilian Burge, Elsie Warilow, 'Buddy' Fisher, and Bill Young. Trimmer's first hospital was in East Street. The new unit was built at Menin Way and is now the Phyllis Tuckwell Hospice.

In 1935 the schoolchildren of the town were invited to a party in Farnham Park to celebrate the Silver Jubilee of King George V and Queen Mary. Each school group wore different coloured ribbon bows pinned to the children and this crowd from East Street School wore pale blue strips on their clothes. Some of the youngsters have badges on their hats with the letters ESS entwined, for the initial letters of their school name.

This group of men from Rowledge and Boundstone, including Farrs, Bonners, Elkins, Stonards, and Cranhams, banded together c. 1908, and cut the padlocks off gates which had been erected by the owners of Alice Holt Forest, to stop people from Rowledge using the footpath to get to Bentley Station. Just as an earlier incident of a similar type at Moor Park, people-power won and the path through the wood remained open from then onwards.

Above: All dressed up in their best bib-and-tucker (and white aprons) are these pupils at Rowledge School in 1913. The headmaster, left, was Tommy Stroud. The children include: Sid Carter, Jack Moss, Frank Farr, Gilbert Moss, Billy Davies, Elsie Swann, Kitty Henwood, Bertha Bryant, Patrick Patterson (whose father was the village cobbler), Bertha Little, Sylvia Bullen, Daisy Farr, Bessie Mason, Kitty Ralph, Flo Parratt, Kitty Knight, Bertha Birmingham and boys of whom only the surnames of three are known, Chiverton, Kemp and Glastonbury.

Right: Winifred Murphy (neé Farr), was given a spinning wheel on this Dorcas Linen float, which was Smyth's entry in a Farnham Carnival, in 1926, to raise money for local good causes. The shop was in East Street and supplied the wherewithal to provide for the large family of Smyth children, Patrick who became a priest (and apparently had a wonderful voice because his mother had laid shamrock on his tongue soon after he was born), Anthony, Peter, Mary, Sarah, Rose, Kathleen, Agnes and Joan. Kathleen (known as Miss Kay), Agnes and Rose ran the shop until its closure on 5 August 1989.

In the days before television, entertainment

in villages, at least, was by way of garden parties, plays on the village hall stage and occasional lantern slide shows. Here the Rowledge Mother's Union, some dressed for an entertainment they were to give, are in the garden of Mrs Lushington's home. Those who can be identified include: Mrs Grimsdale, Mrs Lushington, Mrs Bicknell (who kept the Hare and Hounds), Ellen Farr, Dorothy Swann (who ran the paper shop) and Miss Lane.

Although only a couple of names of players are named in this line-up of Farnham Cricket Club, it is known that they played Liphook, who declared at 214 for 6. For Farnham A. Baker scored 122 before he was out and R.F. Baker made 81 runs thus giving Farnham 217 for 2.

The crowds were out in force in Castle Street in 1897 for the Diamond Jubilee celebrations of Queen Victoria. The plane saplings which can be seen on the left are those planted in front of the almshouses close to the Nelson Arms, to commemorate the day and are still growing well almost a century later.

The saplings in the upper picture can be seen in full growth, below, in this picture which was taken of floats going up Castle Street during the 1970s. Farnham Division of St John Ambulance Brigade, have their ambulance on the right, with a uniformed member standing beside it. The Coach and Horses was then under the Courage livery and Grays Travel, the place where a holiday in the sun could be booked, is extreme left.

Above: Maypole dancing was a traditional event in the past, on May Day each year. In 1913, at Frensham Hill House, just before the First World War began and the building was turned into a hospital, the little girls from Rowledge School, performed to perfection with the multi-coloured ribbons. Their teacher, at the back, was Miss Scotney and the dancers were: Flora Kennedy, Violet Painter, Eva Beacham, Ella Webb, Winnie Farr, Kitty Webb, Marjorie Thomson, Winnie Painter, Connie Rowson, Cecily Edwards, Alice Parratt, Cecily Snook, Dolly Elkins, Alice Mortimer, Bessie Mason, May Little, Elsie Swan.

Left: Although this section is mainly connected with groups, it has often been said that 'two's company' and for Irene Moulsley her horse, on the milk round from Farnham Dairy, was all the company that she needed during her working hours in the Second World War. No doubt her father, the blacksmith in Upper Church Lane, kept the horse well-shod, something which was a necessity with so many ironstone cobbles on the roads, as in this one which is close to the Rectory and opposite the forge.

Every schoolchild in Farnham, in 1935, should be on this picture, possibly the largest crowd ever photographed in the town. It is the party to celebrate the Silver Jubilee of King George V in May 1935, to which every child who attended school was invited to attend. Amateur movie-camera enthusiasts made a film of the week's special activities and this was shown at the old picture palace on 10 June. Chairman Alan Tice had appeared in the film so many times that another well-known townsman, Mr Philipson-Stow asked whether there was any truth in the rumour that Mr Tice had been offered a contract from Hollywood? The picture below is an event in Gostrey Meadow, also for the Silver Jubilee. Mr Tice, mentioned above, is in the foreground in a light suit, watching a lady with a spade who is obviously helping to plant a commemorative tree.

The staff at Blacklidge Bros., high class grocers and provision merchants, at The Bourne, had their photograph taken c.1910. Five young men in long white aprons and short white jackets are on hand to give 'Prompt attention to all orders' as their advertisement read. The one young lady is presumably the cashier and the owner stands in the doorway. The shop also sold mundane articles such as pails, baskets and scrubbing boards.

This group is from Hale School and they are performing a Christmas play. Fairies, soldiers, and pirates all seem to be mingling with a bride and her attendants although there is a notable absence of a bridegroom. Nancy Orchard, who lives in Upper Hale Road, and who for many years worked at Farnham Magistrate's Court office, is one of the cast.

Eleven

By the Wey

In any book of this type there will, inevitably, be many photographs which do not strictly come under any of the prescribed chapter headings. However, as everything in this book appertains to Farnham and its environs, and as the River Wey runs almost exactly through the middle of the area, there is no picture which has been included which was taken farther than three miles away from the Wey. Therefore, By the Wey would seem to link all the remaining pictures neatly together.

Before passing over this page quickly, thinking that it is just another view of the Town Hall Buildings, look again carefully. This is the new Town Hall but it is adjacent to the old Corn Exchange building on the right. Only scaffolding, protruding at first floor level, indicates that soon the brickwork on the right will be pulled down and a new building, with an arcade, making a covered walkway for pedestrians, will be built. The entrance to the National Provincial Bank was in Castle Street and the stone slab beneath which was the conduit for a fresh water supply for the town is about three feet under cover behind the first arch on the right of the corner.

Despite the cheerful faces of the children in the upper picture, these two snapshots, taken in Hale, are connected by health as well as happiness. The children in fancy dress posed on Hale Recreation ground c. 1930 when the building at the back was part of Hale Cottage Hospital. Later this small hospital was changed into three homes for elderly people in the village and they were known as Hale Hospital Cottages. In the 1980s they were sold for private accommodation. The lower picture was taken at the Mary Yolland Home, about 200 yards, as the crow flies, from Hale Hospital Cottages. The building has gone but a close is named after the founder of this sanatorium for girls. A wicker carriage, in which adults could be pushed about, stands at the front of the building. Because Hale and Heath End, like Shortheath and Rowledge, were situated on high ground, they were considered to be healthy places and so there were several sanatoriums there.

It is a century since the Dean family posed for this picture. John and Jane Dean brought up a family of eleven children at Mount Pleasant, where one, eighty-five-year-old Dorothy still lives. Pictured between his parents is Charles. In front of him is Harold holding a small green and black tin train which is still in Dorothy's possession. Elizabeth is on her father's lap and baby Elsie is with her mother. The Deans are one of the most respected families in Farnham, whose members have almost always lived very long lives.

This picture is believed to have been a Hale Women's Institute entry to a carnival between the two World Wars. It was a game of Living Whist and the group is on the grassy area near the old tennis court which used to stand at the side of Hale Institute.

Farnham has been a breeding ground for authors for at least 400 years and it is through writing books that these four people are connected. Top left is novelist Ken Follett, who lived at Tilford for a number of years in the 1980s. He is a supporter of the Labour Party and married the former Barbara Broer from Farnham. Top right is Sir John Verney who, with Tony Crowe, was one of the main supporters of the campaign to save Farnham Maltings. He was an accomplished artist as well as an author. Bottom left is hotelier (at the Bishop's Table) and author Oliver Moxon, who invented a new type of dog lead in 1968 which he hoped would make him a fortune and bottom right is Julian Critchley, author and Member of Parliament for Aldershot for many years, although he lived in Farnham during this time, to the annoyance of his constituents.

Among the workers who made munitions boxes at Crosby's during the Second World War, were a number of good markspeople with rifles. In 1943 Jack Carpenter, Helen Cranstone, Dot Clarke and Dot Gilliam, all of whom are in this photograph, received the cup as the winning Rifle Shooting Team. Helen Cranstone, front row, left, was one of the most conscientious volunteers at Farnham Maltings from the time that it opened until 1992. She had a chair in the Great Hall bought for her, by an anonymous donor, in appreciation of all her voluntary work there and for always having a smile on her face.

Two other people who are seldom seen without a smile are Lord of the Manor, Ken Kent, left, and Alan Taylor of Allamanda Estates. Here the men are shaking hands at the completion of the St Georges development between Bear Lane and Castle Street. Both men have done their best to make sure that all their building work is sympathetic to Farnham's existing old buildings.

Above: The two men and the large bell on this page are connected through music. Top left is Alan Fluck, music master at Farnham Grammar School and the man who, in the 1970s, had a hit musical, *Love on the Dole*, which was performed in many parts of the country as well as London. Above right is David Victor-Smith, a choirmaster of the highest calibre, who has led his group of young people to international fame as well as winning the Sainsbury Youth Choir of the Year competition. In keeping with the mainly nostalgia aspect of this book David's photograph, like that of Alan Fluck, was taken in the 1970s.

Left: There are eight bells in the tower of St. Andrew's Parish Church and in the early 1960s they were re-cast. The bell on the left is the tenor and it weighs almost one ton. It is seen here before being hauled up into the tower once more to provide music at the times of weddings and everyday church services. The familiar tune of 'Life let us cherish, While yet the taper glows, And the fresh flow'ret, Pluck, ere it close', which once rang out every three hours, was immortalized in some of Edna Lyall's books as well as in her introduction to Gordon Home's *Homeland Handbook*, which was published in 1900.

Farnham has many firsts to its credit but two are quite opposite in their sound level. The first two-minute silence has already been mentioned but the 'first' represented by the people above, must, by definition, have plenty of sound. The award-winning *Farnham and Alton Talking Newspaper for the Blind*, the first such paper in the country records four editions each week, from its studio in Farnham Maltings under the organizational skills of Tony Kenchington (John Anthony of BBC Radio). This photograph was taken in the 1980s when national broadcaster, David Jacobs, right, recorded with some of the regular team of volunteers, from left to right: Reg Thompson, Tony Kenchington, Jackie Alliss, Phillip Jay, Col. Courtney, Lady 'Gerry' Bradshaw.

A 'first' of the written, rather than spoken, word is represented above by Charles Hammick, centre, who opened his first bookshop (which later grew into the multi-million pound Hammick empire), in Downing Street, Farnham in 1967. The author Laurie Lee is on the right, signing one of his books.

An interesting trio is featured above from the three major political parties in this country, although on this occasion they were on neutral ground. On the left, Sir Godfrey Nicholson, former Conservative MP for Farnham, is shaking hands with David Lea, assistant general secretary of the TUC while Michael Blower, architect, author and local councillor for the Liberal Democrat party, looks on. The occasion was a visit in 1987 by Sir Godfrey, aged eighty-five years, for the 40th birthday party of the Farnham Society of which he was president. Mr Blower was the chairman at the time of the anniversary.

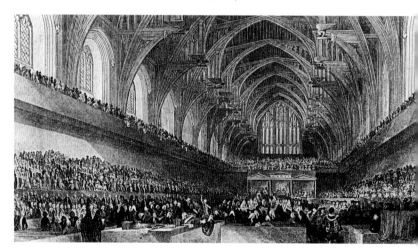

Sir Godfrey Nicholson, in the upper picture, would have been familiar with the sight of these beams in Westminster Hall. This feat of Medieval craftsmanship was constructed in Farnham 600 years ago, in 1395. It was taken, in pieces, by cart and boat, to London and reconstructed to make, what was then, the largest roof structure, without supporting pillars, in Europe.

Although the precise date when this photograph was taken is not known, it is interesting to note that it had to be before 1897 because the plane trees have not yet been planted outside the almshouses to commemorate Queen Victoria's Diamond Jubilee. The almshouses, built in 1619, were intended for the habitation of eight poor, honest, old, impotent people.

This house was demolished to make way for the new Council Offices in South Street, which were officially opened on 13 February 1903. It shows how rural parts of the town still were, at the beginning of the twentieth century, even on the main road to the railway station which was only 400 yards away.

Age, in different forms, connects all seven pictures on this and the facing page. Top left, David Graham, a learned and well-known local archaeologist is in a typical pose, looking down at a 'find' and next to him, top right, is Maurice Elphick, a former President of the Chamber of Commerce and member of the family which owns Elphicks, the shop and departmental store founded in Farnham in 1881, by his grandfather. Antiques join the men in the two bottom pictures. On the right is Ron Putnam who for many years ran a respected antique dealer's shop in Downing Street, until he retired in 1994, and left is Colin Bridgestock, whose antiques' emporium was in Timber Close, opposite the public conveniences from which someone once took the brass covers of urinals and tried to sell them to Mr Bridgestock, saying they were horse brasses!

The building above left was originally a warehouse where hops were bagged. It was owned by a Mr Macdonald who hired out tents to the War Office during the Crimean War. The brickwork beneath the arched areas was knocked out in 1951, by Harold Falkner the town's eccentric architect, who lived opposite this building, and the front referred to below put in. The picture above was probably taken during the Second World War because of the tape on the windows (to stop the glass shattering from bomb blast) and the black and white stripes on the lamp-post. Below, left, is Harold Falkner and below, right, the former Surrey and Hants News building, in 1985, with a front which came from a pastrycook's in The Cornhill, London, built c.1830 but which was demolished in the 1920s.

This unusual view of Bourne Mill, from the Borelli Collection, shows a building to the front of the present one, extending over what is now the pavement, and looking towards the Shepherd and Flock public house in the background. The roundel on the wall of the building has the words 'Caution, dangerous corner' on it. One wonders what a visitor from 75 years ago, coming back today, would have thought of the dangers now, with four lanes of traffic on a roundabout being fed by a fifth lane of cars and lorries at this point. Bourne Mill has been the subject of much newspaper comment in the early 1990s some of it connected with areas of trees which have been felled on the instructions of its current owner. The small, white poles in front of the building still remain, as does the porch over the main door.

Farnham has had some very distinguished residents including William Cobbett, the man who is buried in this tomb beside which stand Elfrida Manning, accompanied by Major Ken Hocking, a former head of the William Cobbett School at Weybourne. Mrs Manning loved Farnham Park and its trees and tried to preserve them for future generations. She also wrote learned works on Farnham's history as well as more whimsical booklets about her own childhood. The two women below have also played major parts in Farnham's social history of the twentieth century.

Marjorie Clemons, left, who was 92 years old when she died in 1992, loved animals more than anything else. She founded BARK animal rescue and although her manner was often offputting to humans she was beloved by every animal with which she came into contact. Gwendoline Beckett, right, who was 100 years old in January 1995 is a former pupil of Farnham Girls' Grammar School, a violinist and was secretary to Sir Adrian Boult, conductor of the BBC Symphony Orchestra, for 28 years.

No book about ordinary people would be complete without a wedding group. Above is the wedding of Frank Hack and Annie Elizabeth Knight, which took place at St. Peter's Church, Wrecclesham on 20 August 1913 and includes Harry Hack, Bert Clark, Jack Wyatt, Jack Hack, George Knight, Liue Hack, Cecil Bartlett, Bert Hack, Daisy Hack, Nell Wyatt, Kate Knight, Alfred Hack, Meg and Alf Wyatt, Jack Knight, Edie Barnard, Dorrie Hack, Doll Clark, Annie Knight.

Seventeen years after the wedding photograph was taken, young Peter Hack, middle, back row, related to the Hacks in the top picture, was photographed in Farnham Park, playing on a tree which had blown down in 1927. With Peter are Dick and Peter Tomlin, Nellie Hawkins, Eileen Hobbs, Margaret Carter and ? Bond.

Each of the men on this page has excelled in a different field in the history of Farnham's population. Henry Liu, top left, is the town's longest-standing restaurateur, having run the Kar Ling Kwong in East Street for more than 30 years. He came to England from Hong Kong and has raised his family here, his elder daughter graduating to become a doctor recently.

Next to him is Sid Towns, formerly of Middle Church Lane, one of the very few men of Farnham who has been allowed to enter the Chelsea Royal Hospital of Pensioners. Bottom right Peter Underwood sits in a contemplative pose. Peter has written more books about ghosts and the supernatural than almost anyone else in this country. He also affirms that he believes Farnham has more ghosts than any other town in Britain.

Harold Cole, one of Farnham's best-known characters, started his working life in 1928. His first, and only job (apart from service with the Royal Corps of Signals during the Second World War), was at the *Farnham Herald* initially working under the paper's founder, Ernest Langham. Through his newspaper work he was able to visit many countries, take trips on maiden voyages of ships and early flights on aeroplanes, meet many famous people including the Ethiopian Emperor Haile Sellasie and attend a number of Royal weddings. He is pictured above as he set out from his home for the wedding of Prince Andrew and Sarah Ferguson. On completion of sixty years working on the newspaper he had both a letter of congratulation and a telephone call from a lady-in-waiting, on behalf of Queen Elizabeth, the Queen Mother. Harold, born and educated at Tilford and living in this area all his life, has probably broadcast the name of the town of Farnham, by word-of-mouth, to more people in the world than anyone else.

Many famous and not-so-famous people have been pictured, and recalled, in this volume which is about Farnham's past. It is however, the babies of today who grow to be the adults of tomorrow who will shape the town at the beginning of the 21st century. In the photograph above, a small child is being held outside Trusler's hardware shop at the entrance to Lower Church Lane, almost 100 years ago, and below is a class of children in an unknown Farnham school taken at about the same time. The unknown and unnamed have always played as much a part in forming the town's history as those people who have hit the headlines. As a postscript dedication this book is to give my appreciation to all the 'unknown' people of Farnham who have lived, worked and died here and each of whom has played a part, however small the way, in shaping its history.

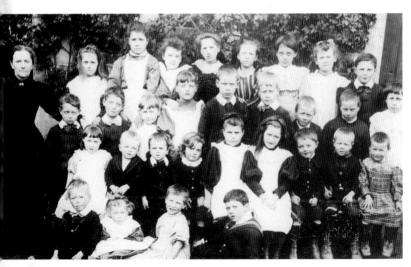

Acknowledgements

In a book of this type it is impossible to locate every photographer – many of the pictures being snapshots of groups, none of whom is now alive. Other pictures have been taken by freelance and staff photographers of both the *Surrey and Hants News* and the *Farnham Herald*. Acknowledgement is given to them, where known, and also to the past editors of both newspapers. I apologize to anyone who finds their name has been missed out but I can assure them that without their eye for a good picture this book would not have been complete. Individually I should like to thank Dame Vera Lynn, Peter Underwood, Eddie Trusler, Wendy Hobart, Nellie Hawkins, Harold Cole, Vic Burge, Kay Crowe, Win Murphy, Richard Dyer, Chris Shepheard, Rosalind Crowe, Rosanne Croly, Annette Booth, Terence Pepper, John Price, Maurice Hewins, Tim Humphrey, Nancy Orchard, Mrs D. Orchard, Peggy Abrahams, Irene Conley, Caryl Griffith, Stan Winslade, Margaret Bide, Helen Cranstone, Mark Parratt, Ron Moffatt, Josie Nicholls, Margaret Mullery, Maurice Elphick, Clem Keddie, Yvonne Moore, Keith Hawkins, Mrs Dorothy Dimes, Mrs Quita Kirk-Duncan, Ken Kent, Gillian Drew at the Surrey Archaeological Society, Anne Jones and the Museum of Farnham's Borelli Collection for pictures on P10(L), P13(U), P20(U), P23(L), P35, P36(L), P37(U&L), P43(U&L), P45(U), P66(U&L), P67(U&L), P68(L), P70, P71(U), P74(L), P75(U&L), P78(U), P79(U), P80(U&L), P89, P90(U), P91(U), P92, P94, P98, P99(L), P107(U), P111, P112(L), P121(U), Dennis Stone of the Farnham Herald for photographs on P12(L), P15(L), P21, P25(U), P29(U), P30, P32(U), P39, P83, P84, P116(L) and the late Dr Tony Crowe, Bill Ewbank-Smith and Edward Griffith. all of whom have died in the last few years. Finally I should like to thank my husband, Ted, for all his help in the production of this book.